*Freemasonry in the Medieval
or Middle Ages*

By

Robert I. Clegg
& C. W. Leadbeater

Copyright © 2020 Lamp of Trismegistus. All rights reserved. No part of this publication may be reproduced or transmitted in any form or by any means, electronic or mechanical, including photocopying, recording, or by any information storage and retrieval system, without permission in writing from Lamp of Trismegistus. Reviewers may quote brief passages.

ISBN: 978-1-63118-450-5

Foundations of Freemasonry Series

Other Books in this Series and Related Titles

The Two Great Pillars of Boaz and Jachin
by Albert G. Mackey &c (978-1-63118-433-8)

The Lost Keys of Freemasonry or The Secret of Hiram Abiff
by Manly P. Hall (978-1-63118-427-7)

The Mysteries of Freemasonry & the Druids
by Albert G. Mackey, Manly P. Hall, &c (978-1-63118-444-4)

Royal Arch, Capitular and Cryptic Masonry
by various authors (978-1-63118-425-3)

Masonic Symbolism of Easter and the Christ in Masonry
by various authors (978-1-63118-434-5)

Masonic Symbolism of King Solomon's Temple
by Albert G. Mackey &c (978-1-63118-442-0)

The Regius Poem or Halliwell Manuscript
by King Solomon (978-1-63118-447-5)

Masonic Life of George Washington
by Albert G. Mackey (978-1-63118-457-4)

Masonic Symbolism of the Apron & the Altar
by various authors (978-1-63118-428-4)

The Kabbalah of Masonry & Related Writings
by W. W. Westcott, Eliphas Levi &c (978-1-63118-453-6)

Symbolism and Discourses on the Entered Apprentice, Fellowcraft and Master Mason Blue Lodge Degrees by various (978-1-63118-413-0)

The Story and Legend of Hiram Abiff by William Harvey, Manly P. Hall & Albert G. Mackey (978-1-63118-411-6)

Audio Versions are also Available on Audible and iTunes

Table of Contents

Introduction...7

Freemasonry and Monasticism in the Middle Ages
by Robert I. Clegg...9

Craft Masonry in Medieval Times
by C. W. Leadbeater
Part I: Evolutionary Methods...19
Part II: The Withdrawal of the Mysteries...23
Part III: The Christian Mysteries...25
Part IV: The Repression of the Mysteries...29
Part V: The Crossing of Traditions...31
Part VI: The Two Lines of Descent...33
Part VII: The Culdees...35
Part VIII: Celtic Christianity in Britain...37
Part IX: The Druidic Mysteries...39
Part X: The Holy Grail...41
Part XI: Heredom...43

Operative Masonry in the Middle Ages
by C. W. Leadbeater
Part I: The Temporary Custodians...47
Part II: Decline of the Collegia...49
Part III: The Comacini...51
Part IV: The Comacine Lodges...55
Part V: Other Survivals of the Collegia...57
Part VI: The Compagnonnage...59
Part VII: The Stonemasons of Germany...63
Part VIII: The English Guilds...65
Part IX: The Rise of Gothic Architecture...67
Part X: The Old Charges...73

Introduction

From the beginning of Modern Freemasonry's birthdate of 1717, the intelligentsia of humanity have found refuge for safe reflection within the walls of the fraternity. Masonic writers have produced a nearly incalculable amount of written musings on a multitude of esoteric and philosophical subjects, as they relate to the ancient mysteries that Freemasonry currently storehouses. Sadly, most of it appears to have sat largely unread, as American Freemasonry in particular, continues to transform itself into something that bears little resemblance to what it was originally designed to be. The true essence of Freemasonry is not that of blind patriotism or a single-minded national religion but one of Universal Brotherhood and altruism, designed for the betterment not just of its members but of society as a whole. In particular, for those who are not members of the fraternity, as Freemasonry has always acted as a beacon, to help guide humanity through darker times, with the hopes that one day we will collectively reach a truly enlightened age.

It's not uncommon for new members joining the fraternity to find little education within the walls of many modern lodges, in spite of so much written material available to the membership. Many older members are not simply uneducated with regards to real Masonic history and symbology, not to mention the vast arena of related subjects, but they are disinterested in all of it, as well.

Lamp of Trismegistus is doing its part to help preserve humanity's Masonic history by making some of these classics available to those students who are seeking to unearth the knowledge of these ancient colossi. As such, Lamp of Trismegistus offers its readers highlights of Masonic study, culled from a variety of authors and viewpoints, with the hope bringing education back into the fraternity. So, be sure to check out other titles in our *Foundations of Freemasonry Series* as well as our *Esoteric Classics, Theosophical Classics, Occult Fiction, Paranormal Classics, Supernatural Fiction* and our *Christian Apocrypha Series*, and don't be afraid to let a little altruism into your own heart or even into your Lodge. You can also download the audio versions of most of these titles from iTunes or Audible, for learning on the go.

Freemasonry and Monasticism in the Middle Ages

By Robert I. Clegg

There are some old documents known to us, as the Ancient Charges. These show that the Freemasons of the middle ages possessed a curious tradition peculiar to themselves. This tradition dealt with the origin of Masonry and the invention of geometry, that branch of the liberal arts and sciences that enters so largely into the practice of the craft whether operative or speculative. Conder, in his book, "The Hole Craft and Fellowship of Masons," says that, "this tradition was without doubt largely due to the clerical influence exercised over their calling."

Not only is this very probable but there is internal evidence to indicate that the oldest of these Ancient Charges was written by one holding office in the Church.

This contact of the Lodge and the Church is not surprising. From the most remote antiquity Masons have built structures to house the worshipers of the Deity. At all stages of the work they have been associated with the priesthood. They were also intimately allied with those religious orders affiliated with the Church.

This fact is of itself sufficient to account for the semi-religious body that the Masons became. It explains the moral teaching and the curious traditions found embedded so intimately within the Masonic organization, which has so freely drawn upon the sacred books of the Church and from legendary history.

Brother Conder says further: "*Undoubtedly such was the fact. It is therefore without surprise that about the end of the fourteenth or early in the fifteenth century we find a document, evidently founded on a much earlier one (or on remote oral traditions) which recites the supposed history of the Fellowship of Masons, and lays down rules for the guidance of its members; at the same time inculcating a behavior and conduct, which if not a gratuitous insertion is as regards to ordinary workmen, greatly in advance of the spirit of the time, and far beyond that practiced by the other trades. No doubt this was to support the craft in maintaining its ancient worthy position, and in order that its members might continue to hold their ancient and honorable station.*"

"*As the beauty of the so-called Gothic architecture advanced under the wing of the Church, schools of Masonry, wherein the elements of Euclid were taught to the higher classes of operative masons, became attached to certain religious houses and from time to time efficient workmen left these schools for work further afield.*"

Not only in their structural designs but in the decoration of their buildings the old craftsmen made liberal employment of the principles set forth by the great geometrician, Euclid. In the construction of the equilateral triangle entering into the very first proposition of Euclid's famous "Elements" there was shown to the Master Mason a new form for the arch, a suggestion for the familiar trifold representative of the Trinity, and by the intersection of the circles he was symbolically shown "the Deity ever present where the eternity of the past overlapped the eternity of the future, who was, and is, and is to be."

"If we follow the details of Gothic architecture, we shall see that the triangle and the circle form the keystone to that ornamental tracery for which this style is noted. This symbolical language of Masonry, together with the use of the Mason's square and compasses, would doubtless be used by the ecclesiastics as an object lesson to the workmen engaged on the sacred edifice and so become incorporated in the traditions of their gild. The Masons at the cathedrals and other large ecclesiastical buildings were attached to the monastery, and often a technical school of Masonry was founded by the monks who in teaching the craft would not forget the higher or symbolical meaning to be derived from the geometrical figures used in tracing sections, etc." Thus far I quote Brother Conder.

How far is this vision borne out by the facts? To my mind it has a very reasonable foundation. Let us take but one of the old monastic orders and compare it with Freemasonry. I will not now take the time or space to go carefully into a comparison of the Ancient Charges or any part of them with the rules and regulations laid down by any order of monks. Such a comparison while interesting is largely unnecessary because for all practical purposes the monitorial charges of today are similar to those given in the old charges. You may therefore compare for yourselves what I may say of any monastic institution and determine how far it resembles the Freemasonry that is known to you by its distinctive charges and ceremonies, by our authorized and familiar monitor and ritual.

We will, if you please, consider then the order of St. Benedict. That great lawgiver, dying in the year 542, saw one night in a vision the whole world gathered together under one beam of the sun. So states Gregory in the following century and the tale has come down the long years. In the light of this very suggestive illumination his followers had great breadth in religious convictions.

Said the Venerable Bede: "*You know, my brother, the custom of the Roman Church in which you remember you were bred up. But it pleases me that if you have found anything either in the Roman or the Gallican, or any other Church, which may be more acceptable to Almighty God, you carefully make choice of the same, and sedulously teach the Church of the English, which as yet is new in the Faith, whatsoever you can gather from the several Churches. For things are not to be loved for the sake of places, but places for the sake of good things. Choose therefore from every Church those things that are pious, religious, and upright, and when you have, as it were, made them up into one body, let the minds of the English be accustomed thereto.*" Such were the instructions of Gregory to Augustine.

Newman has given us in the Mission of St. Benedict to Europe an estimate so richly colored by his affectionate regard for the brethren that it reads with extravagant force.

"*Silent men were observed about the country, or discovered in the forest digging, cleaning, and building; and other silent men, not seen, were sitting in the cold cloister tiring their eyes and keeping their attention on the stretch, while they painfully deciphered, then copied and recopied, the manuscripts which they had saved. There was no one that contended or cried out, or drew attention to what was going on; but by degrees the woody swamp became a hermitage, a religious house, a farm, an abbey, a village, a seminary, a school of learning, and a city. Roads and villages connected it with other abbeys and cities which had similarly grown up; and what the haughty Alaric or fierce Attila had broken to pieces these patient meditative men have brought together and made to live again. And then, when they had in the course of many years gained their peaceful victories, perhaps some new invaders came, and with fire and sword undid their slow and persevering toil in an hour. Down in the dust lay the labor and civilization of centuries- - churches, colleges, cloisters, libraries --and nothing was left to them but to begin all over again; but this they did without grudging, so promptly, cheerfully, and tranquilly, as if it were by some law of nature that the restoration came; and they were like the flowers and shrubs and great trees which they reared, and which when ill-treated do not take vengeance or remember evil, but give forth fresh branches, leaves and blossoms, perhaps in greater profusion or with richer quality, for the very reason that the old were rudely broken off."*

Of Dunstan, whose work in the restoration after the ravages of war was notable, Newman recites: *"As a religious he showed himself in the simple character of a Benedictine. He had a taste for the arts generally, especially music. He painted and embroidered; his skill in smith's work is recorded in the well-known legend of his combat with the evil one. And, as the monks of Hilarion joined gardening with psalmody, and Bernard and his Cistercians joined field work with meditation, so did St. Dunstan use music and painting as directly expressive or suggestive of devotion. 'He excelled in writing, painting, molding in wax, carving in wood and bone, and in work in gold, silver, iron, and brass,' says the author of his life in Surius, 'and he used his skill in musical instruments to charm away from himself and others their secular annoyances, and to raise them to the theme of heavenly harmony, both by the sweet words with which he accompanied his airs and by the concord of the airs themselves."*

We are told that when a young man desired to enter the monastery of St. Augustine he had to remain for some time in the guest house as a postulant. When the day was fixed for the admission, or as it was called, the "rastura," the shaving of his head, the prior gave him notice that three days before he was to dine with the abbot. The abbot would then call the prior and two of the seniors, and they appointed the novice- master who was charged to instruct him in all that was necessary for his state, and to supply all his wants. The abbot, then, after some kind words, left the youth in the hands of the master, who examined him and found out if he had everything he wanted for the time of his probation.

The postulant was then warned to cleanse his soul by confession if necessary, and was then instructed in the rudiments of monastic ceremonial. These instructions were spread over the intervening days on one of which the postulant dined with the prior.

On the day appointed the postulant attended divine service and made an offering after the reading of the Gospel. His master then took him to the chapel and there prepared him diligently for the ceremony.

When the hour arrived he went with his master into the chapter house where the brethren were assembled and prostrated himself before the abbot.

He was then asked what he desired and he replied in the usual form. He was then bidden to arise, and was told by the abbot how hard and trying was the life that he desired.

Then he was asked if he was freeborn. Was he in good health and free from any incurable disease? Was he ready to accept hardships as well as pleasant things, to obey and bear ignominy for the love of Christ? To these questions he replied "Yes, by the grace of God."

Continuing the examination the abbot asked if the postulant had ever been professed in any other stricter order; whether he was bound by any promise of marriage, and was he free from debt and irregularity.

On receiving an answer in the negative the abbot granted his prayer; and he was forthwith taken by the novice-master to have his head shaved and be invested with the monastic habit.

Gould gives us the essentials of the initiation into the order of St. Benedict as "The vow was to be made with all possible solemnity, in the chapel, before the relics in the shrine, with the abbot and all the brethren standing by, and once made it was to be irrevocable."

He further points out the relation of the ritual to darkness as connected with death and initiation. Upon the matter of the ceremonial he had the advantage of quoting directly from a communication sent to him by an eyewitness, and which was given in the following terms:

"St. Pauls without the walls of Rome is a basilica church, and in the apse behind the high altar another altar had been fitted up. The head of the Benedictines is a mitered abbot. On this morning the abbot was sitting as I entered the church, with his miter on his head and crozier in hand. Soon after our entrance a young man was led up to the abbot who placed a black cowl on his head. The young man then descended the steps, went upon his knees, put his hands as in the act of prayer, when each of the monks present came up and, also on their knees, kissed him in turn. When they had finished, a velvet cloth, with gold or silver embroidery on it, was spread in front of the altar; on this the young man lay down and a black silk pall was laid over him. Thus, under semblance of a state of death he lay while mass was celebrated by the abbot. When this was finished, one of the deacons of the mass approached where the young man lay, and muttered a few words from a book he held in his hand. I understood that the words used were from the Psalms, and were to this effect: 'Oh thou that sleepest, arise to everlasting life.' The man then arose, was led to the altar, where I think he received the sacrament, and then took his place among the Brotherhood."

The significant numbers three, five and seven, are curiously found to be employed by the Benedictines. There were "three voices" to be recognized among the brethren in the chapter. These were the ones of the accuser, the answerer, and the judge.

Another "five voices" were those of him who presided, the guardians of the order; the precentor and succentor; the brothers charged with keeping the silence, "because silence is called the key of the whole order"; and then the almoner and sub-almoner. These five in their order were the first to proclaim anyone who through their respective offices they knew had infringed the rules. The monk so proclaimed had to go out into the center of the chapter and prostrating made confession of his fault, and saying "Mea culpa" (I have done wrong) and promising amendment then received penance and rebuke.

Everyone who had ceased to be under ward had a right to speak in the chapter on "three points"; defects in the public worship, the breaking of silence, and the distribution of alms. On all other subjects he must ask leave to speak.

In processions there was to be preserved a distance of "seven" feet between each of the monks.

But sufficient has been pointed out to serve our purpose. These extracts will be found highly suggestive to the thoughtful Mason and will recall much that is bound up in his own experience.

Craft Masonry in Medieval Times
by C. W. Leadbeater
Part I:
Evolutionary Methods

The theory of human evolution ordinarily put before us is that of a slow upward progress of man from extremely primitive and almost animal conditions through the Stone Age, the Bronze Age, the Iron Age, until he has arrived at his present level, which is by this hypothesis the highest which he has yet attained. This view is only partially true; it is only on the one hand in a very broad and general sense covering a development lasting many millions of years, and on the other in a purely local sense affecting one or two sub-races, that it can be said to be true at all, for it leaves entirely out of account some of the most important factors in the case.

Let no one ever doubt that evolution is a fact - that God has a plan for man, and that that plan is one of eternal advancement and unfoldment, carrying him on to heights of glory and splendour of which at present we have no conception.

Yet we doubt not through the ages one eternal purpose runs.

And the thoughts of men are widened with the process of the suns. (*Locksley Hall, by Lord Tennyson.*)

But if we wish to understand anything of this wondrous scheme we must begin by trying to grasp its general principles. First, it is no mere haphazard growth; it is being definitely directed from behind by a body of perfected men which we call the Great White Brotherhood - a body which exists to carry out the will of the Logos of the solar system. It works through machinery so vast and complicated that from the physical plane we can never see more than a tiny corner of its operation, and so we constantly misconceive and underrate it.

Secondly, its method of working is cyclical. The soul of man grows by occupying a succession of bodies, each of which is born, grows slowly to maturity, lives its life, learns (or fails to learn) its lesson, and then dies. Just so humanity grows by incarnating in a succession of races, each of which passes through its stage of youth, adolescence, full manhood and decay. Often the period of decay seems sad, both with the man and with the race; often the student of history cannot but regret the passing of a once mighty and splendid civilization to make way for a savagery possibly more virile, but certainly in its youth coarser and cruder.

A flagrant example of that was the destruction of the gentle and beautiful civilization of Peru by the incredibly cruel and atrocious methods of the invading Spaniards; another very similar case was the utterly unjustifiable attack upon the civilization of Rome by the ferocious hordes of Goths and Vandals from the north. So coarse, so brutal were they that their very names have become a proverb, and we use them today to indicate the extremes of clumsiness and wanton destruction. Yet they also were an instrument in the hand of the divine power, and their crass ignorance contained within itself the seed of certain qualities which were in danger of dying out and being forgotten among the decaying races which they were destined to leaven and partially to replace.

Part II:
The Withdrawal of the Mysteries

Even before the destruction of the Roman Empire the withdrawal of the Mysteries as public institutions had taken place; and this fact was mainly due to the excessive intolerance displayed by the Christians. Their amazing theory that none but they could be "saved" from the hell which they themselves had invented naturally led them to try all means, even the most cruel and diabolical persecutions, to force people of other faiths to accept their particular shibboleth. As the Mysteries were the heart and stronghold of a more rational belief, they of course opposed them bitterly, quite forgetful that in the earlier days of their religion they had claimed to possess as much of the inner knowledge as any other system.

Part III:
The Christian Mysteries

Even today it is quite commonly thought that Christianity had no mysteries, and some of its followers boast that in it nothing is hidden. That mistaken idea has been so sedulously impressed upon the world that it leads many people to feel a certain distaste for the wiser faiths which met all needs, and to think of them as unnecessarily hiding part of the truth or grudging it to the world. In the old days there was no such thought as this; it was recognized that only those who came up to a certain standard of life were fit to receive the higher instruction, and those who wished for it set to work to qualify themselves for it. Knowledge is power, and people must prove their fitness before they will be entrusted with power; for the object of the whole scheme is human evolution, and the interests of evolution would not be served by promiscuous publication of occult truth.

Those who maintain the above-mentioned opinion about Christianity are unacquainted with the history of the Church. Though many of the early Christian writers are bitterly hostile to the Mysteries, they indignantly deny the suggestion that in their Church they have nothing worthy of that name, and claim that their Mysteries are in every way as good and deep and far-reaching as those of their 'pagan' opponents. S. Clement says: "He who has been purified in baptism and then initiated into the little Mysteries (has acquired, that is to say, the habits of self-control and reflection), becomes ripe for the greater Mysteries, for Epopteia or Gnosis, the scientific knowledge of God." (*Quoted in Some Glimpses of Occultism, Ch. ii.*) The same writer also said: "It is not lawful to reveal to profane persons the Mysteries of the Logos."

Origen, the most brilliant and learned of all the ecclesiastical Fathers, also asserts the existence of the secret teaching of the Church, and speaks plainly of the difference between the ignorant faith of the undeveloped multitude, and the higher and reasonable faith which is founded upon definite knowledge. He draws a distinction between "the popular irrational faith" which leads to what he calls "somatic Christianity" (the merely physical form of the religion) and the "spiritual Christianity" offered by the Gnosis or wisdom. He makes it perfectly clear that by "somatic Christianity" he means that faith which is based on the gospel history. He says of it: "What better method could be devised to assist the masses?" In Dean Inge's Christian Mysticism he is quoted as teaching that:

The Gnostic or sage no longer needs the crucified Christ. The eternal or spiritual gospel which is his possession shows clearly all things concerning the Son of God Himself both the Mysteries shown by his words and the things of which his acts were the symbols ... Origen regards the life, death and resurrection of Christ as only one manifestation of a universal law, which was really enacted not in this fleeting world of shadows, but in the eternal counsels of the Most High. He considers that those who are thoroughly convinced of the universal truths revealed by the incarnation and the atonement need trouble themselves no more about their particular manifestations in time. (*Op. cit., p. 89.*)

Here we see distinct and repeated references to the hidden teaching, greater far than anything known to the Church of the present day, and carrying those who study it to a much higher level than is ever now attained by the disciples of orthodoxy. What has become of this magnificent heritage of Christianity? It is true that everything the Church knows is now given out, but that is only because she has forgotten the mysteries which she used to keep hidden. This is one of the principal reasons why she has lost control of her more intellectual sons, and has therefore failed in her duty to educate and instruct the people in the most important things of life, and has left our age the most unpractical one ever known.

We have come into this world to live our lives, not to make money, and on the way in which we live depends the condition of our future births. One would think, therefore, that people would be taught all about these things in school. It is certain that everyone must die, but nobody tells us anything that is worth knowing about that important matter. On the contrary, exoteric Christianity in the days of its power positively forbade those who knew to say anything on the subject, and enforced with the most terrible weapons its incredibly foolish commandment: "Thou shalt not think."

Happily all this wonderful wisdom is not lost, for much of it is preserved to us in the teachings of Freemasonry. There were many thousands of people at the time when Christianity began to dominate the world who still clung to the ancient tradition, who preferred to state their views in the older forms. As Christianity grew narrower and more aggressive, and less tolerant of fact, those who knew something of the truth, and wished to preserve its enshrinement in those older forms, had more and more to keep their meetings secret; for the Church was exceedingly intolerant towards anyone who dared to differ from her, even in minor matters.

Part IV:
The Repression of the Mysteries

In A.D. 399 the Emperor Theodosius issued his celebrated edict, which was a heavy blow to the outer manifestation of the ancient pagan faith:

Whatever privileges were conceded by the ancient laws to the priests, ministers, prefects, hierophants of sacred things, or by whatsoever name they may be designated, are to be abolished henceforth, and let them not think that they are protected by a granted privilege when their religious confession is known to have been condemned by the law.

By A.D. 423 the penalties against those who clung to the old beliefs had become severe, for in a later edict of the same Emperor we find:

Although the pagans that remain ought to be subjected to capital punishment if at any time they are detected in the abominable sacrifices of demons, let exile and confiscation of goods be their punishment. (*Codex Theodosianus XVI, 10, 14, 23, quoted in A Source Book for Ancient Church History. Ayer, p. 371.*)

Wherever possible the temples of the gods were destroyed, the ancient libraries were burnt, the statues and other relics were broken in pieces by the brutal hands of the savage Christians - and what destruction remained to be accomplished in the Western Empire was completed by the no less barbarian invaders. So perished the outer worship of the gods of Greece and Rome; the Mysteries were withdrawn into inviolable secrecy, which remained unbroken until after the Reformation, when the Church had lost her power to burn and torture all who did not at least pretend to be in agreement with her doctrines.

Part V:
The Crossing of Traditions

This retirement took place in several countries simultaneously, so several traditions arose which, like the mystery-systems from which they were derived, differed considerably in their details, though they were always based upon a common plan. These traditions have crossed and recrossed one another constantly throughout the centuries, have influenced each other in all sorts of secret ways, have been carried from country to country by many messengers; so that the Masonry which emerged in the eighteenth century bears the signature of many lines of descent, of many interacting schools of mystical philosophy.

Behind all these different movements, utterly unknown except by the few disciples charged with the work of keeping alight the sacred fire during the Dark Ages, stood the White Lodge itself, encouraging all that was good in them, guiding and inspiring all who were willing to open themselves to such influence.

By efflux of time the true philosophy has gradually faded out of them again and again, and from time to time the adepts have taken advantage of some favourable opportunity to restore a little of it sometimes by founding a new rite or school, sometimes by instigating the establishment of additional degrees in an existing rite. We see, therefore, a number of parallel and equally valid streams of tradition running down in secret throughout the Middle Ages, and emerging here and there in movements which are to some extent known in the outer world. The real continuum of Masonry may thus be compared to the roots of a plant creeping along under the ground, and giving forth apparently separate plants at intervals. There are, however, more or less broken lines of outward descent that may be traced up to a certain point on the physical plane; it is with these that we shall especially concern ourselves in the following chapters.

Part VI:
The Two Lines of Descent

We have already indicated that the only portion of the Masonic tradition which was anciently divided into definite degrees is that which we now call Craft or symbolic Masonry - the direct descendant of the Lesser and the Greater Mysteries of Egypt and Judaea, and closely akin to the Mysteries of Greece. Greater sacramental powers were conferred and deeper spiritual instruction was given to the few who were endeavouring to prepare themselves for the true Mysteries of the White Lodge; but these cannot be called degrees after the manner of Craft Masonry, for even in ancient Egypt they were not organized as such. Both these lines of succession passed down through the Middle Ages; the Craft degrees were deliberately confused with operative building, and were thus transmitted, although in secrecy, in the outer world, but the higher instruction still belonged only to the few, and was handed down in far deeper secrecy still, being introduced from time to time into the heart of various mystical schools, which were much more exclusive in their choice of members than the operative builders.

With the Craft degrees were associated the kernel of those ceremonies which we now attach to the Honourable Degree of Mark Master Mason, connected, as always, with the 2°, and the Supreme Order of the Holy Royal Arch of Jerusalem, worked in conjunction with the 3°. Our present rituals for these are not therefore necessarily ancient, for all have been subjected to much modern recasting and editing. A body of legend and tradition explanatory of the ceremonial appears also to have been handed down; and the relics of this have in comparatively recent times been manufactured into separate ceremonial degrees - such, for example, as certain of the earlier stages of the Ancient and Accepted Scottish Rite, and their kindred among the side or additional degrees worked in England and America.

Part VII:
The Culdees

A noteworthy line of tradition, connected with Craft Masonry to some extent, but even more with the Royal Order of Scotland and the 18°, is found among the Culdees of Ireland, Scotland and York. Few trustworthy sources of information exist concerning them, though they have been the centre of many beautiful dreams; but they are thought by scholars to have been either an ancient monastic order with settlements in Ireland and Scotland, (*Enc. Brit., Art. Culdees, Eleventh Ed.*) or in a wider sense to have represented the monks and clerics of the Celtic Church without limitation, as well as those understood to be their successors in later times. (*Hist. Freemasonry, R. F. Gould, Vol. I, p. 47.*)

We hear of them in Ireland from the ninth to the seventeenth centuries; from the ninth to the fourteenth centuries in Scotland, where they had several influential monastic communities, including one upon the holy island of Iona, which had been one of the greatest spiritual centres of Celtic Christianity long before the word Culdee is mentioned in the historical records concerning it. In Wales in the twelfth century there was a strict community of Culdees living in the island of Bardsey, the holy island of Wales; while in England we find them as officiating clergy in the Cathedral Church of S. Peter at York during the reign of King Athelstan, who was so closely linked with English Masonic tradition. (*Hist. Freemasonry, R. F. Gould, Vol. I, p. 50 ff.*) It is said that after requesting the prayers of the Culdees for victory over the Scots, when he was successful he granted them a perpetual endowment of corn, to enable them to continue their works of charity.

Their name has been derived from the Celtic Cele-De, meaning Companion or Servant of God, and from the Latin Colidei, worshippers of God; others have thought that it came from the Celtic cuill dich, meaning men of seclusion; but the etymology of the word is not certainly known. Godfrey Higgins claimed that the word Culdee was the same as Chaldee, and ascribed to them an Oriental origin, although he adduces no authentic evidence for his views. (*Quoted by Bro. A. E. Waite: A New Encyclopaedia of Freemasonry, Art. Culdees.*)

Part VIII:
Celtic Christianity in Britain

Students of English Church History know that Christianity was introduced into Great Britain long before the missions of S. Patrick and S. Augustine; and there has been a persistent feeling that this Christianity was not that of Rome, but had affinities rather with the Eastern rites. (*Neander, General History of the Christian Religion and Church, Vol. i. p. 117. Quoted Gould, loc. cit.*) Many traditions, none of them substantiated by authentic records, bear witness to this belief, and point the way to a truth in the background. There is the beautiful legend of Joseph of Arimathaea and the Holy Thorn of Glastonbury; there is the story told by Theodoret and Fortunatus that S. Paul visited Britain, which appears to receive some confirmation from S. Clement of Rome; while Eusebius, the great ecclesiastical historian, mentions that some of the twelve apostles visited the British Isles. (*Foundation Stones. Austin Clare, p. 16.*) Indeed it was not until the twelfth century that Celtic Christianity was finally brought into line with the usages of Roman Catholicism. (*Enc. Brit., loc. cit.*)

The holy island of Iona, once the heart of the old Celtic Church, lies off the west coast of Scotland among the Inner Hebrides. It was called Hy or Icolmkill (the island of Columba of the Church), and by the Highlanders Innis nan Druidhneah (the isle of the Druids), implying that before the coming of S. Columba in A.D. 563 it had been a hallowed centre of the ancient worship of the Celts. (*Enc. Brit., Art. Iona.*) The monks of Iona spread their learning over Sootland and Northern England, and the early Celtic Bishops owned the abbot of Iona as their spiritual head. In 717 the monks of Iona were expelled from Scotland by the Pictish King Nechtan; but their place was largely filled by the Culdees of Ireland, (*Enc. Brit., Art. Culdees.*) who appear to have been followers of the same tradition. No mention is made of the Culdees in Scotland after A.D. 1382. (*Gould, loc. cit.*)

We find that the early British Church, of which the Culdees were the later survivors, possessed a beautiful and mystical form of Christianity derived from Eastern sources and closely connected with the traditions of the Essenes, who were the immediate followers of Our Lord. It had the apostolic succession of the Christian Church, but its teachings were less defined and rigid, more mystical and poetic than the Roman scholasticism which in later days so completely absorbed it. In addition to the Christian sacraments, certain secret rites were brought to Britain by the original missionaries, rites belonging to the Mithraic line of succession, which, as we have already seen, were practiced among the Essenes; and there may also in all likelihood have existed among them a succession of Jewish Masonry unconnected with the Roman Collegia.

Part IX:
The Druidic Mysteries

These various lines of tradition were assimilated to some extent with the indigenous Mysteries of the Druids, which, however, had lost much of the splendour of former times; and even the outer Christian rites became touched with that peculiar beauty which is the heritage of the Celt. We find confirmation of the ancient legend that the splendid Celtic race called the Tuatha De Danaan, which flourished in ancient Ireland, came originally from Greece through Scandinavia; and the same is true of other offshoots of the Celtic stock which settled in Wales, Cornwall and Brittany. They all formed a branch of that Fourth Sub-race from which the later Greeks and Romans were also descended; and the origin of the Mysteries of the Druids may be traced to the great World Teacher, in His incarnation as Orpheus, the singer of Hellas, though they were also influenced somewhat by the still older Mysteries of Ireland which date from Atlantean times. The lyre of Apollo became the harp of Angus; and the old worship of God as the divine beauty manifesting through music thus passed down into Britain.

The Druidical Mysteries had a certain influence on the imported Roman or Norman rites. They are compared by Strabo and Artemidorus to the rites of Samothrace, and by Dionysius to those of Bacchus, while Mnaseas refers to their Kabiric correspondences. We learn from Diogenes Laertius and from Caesar that the Druidic method of instruction was by symbols, enigmas and allegories, and that they taught orally, deeming it unlawful to commit their knowledge to writing. It is said that their ceremonies of initiation required much physical purification and mental preparation. In the first degree the aspirant's symbolical death was represented, and in the third his regeneration from the womb of the giant goddess Ceridwin and the committal of the newly-born to the waves in a small boat, symbolical of the ark. Their doctrines were similar to those of Pythagoras - including reincarnation and the existence of one Supreme Being. Apart from a few stray references in classical authors, we know of them today chiefly through the Bardic songs attributed to the Welsh poet Taliesin, of the sixth century A.D., who claimed Druidic initiation. Culdees of York blended Christian mysticism with these pre-Christian rites, and so linked them with modern Masonry.

There have been many other mysteries, such as those of Ireland, closely connected with the Druids, and of Scandinavia, wherein the death and resurrection of Balder was the chief theme, and no doubt all these were connected with the source of our present Masonry, being branches of the same tree, even though external traces of their relationship in the past have disappeared.

Part X:
The Holy Grail

As part of this indirect heritage from the Greek Mysteries came the well-known symbol of the Krater or Cup, which in the intermingling with early British Christianity was identified with the Sangreal, the Chalice used by our Lord at the Last Supper for the founding of the Holy Eucharist. King Arthur, who has often been supposed to be an imaginary hero, was a very real and most lovable and sagacious ruler, of whom England may well be proud; his Round Table also is fact and not fiction, and among its Knights there was a rite of the Christian Mysteries centring round the beautiful story of the quest for the Holy Grail. Some there were who took the legend literally and undertook endless physical-plane pilgrimages in search of an earthly cup; others knew that the mystical meaning of the finding of the Holy Grail is the union between the higher and the lower self, which is one of the qualifications for initiation into the true Mysteries of the White Lodge; for the Chalice symbolically represents the causal body into which the "blood" of the Mystery is poured. "I am the cup, His love the wine." The Mysteries of the Holy Grail were simultaneously celebrated in various centres, both in Great Britain and on the Continent, where they doubtless became mingled with other lines of tradition; and in them we find clear traces of one of those secret schools in which the flame of the hidden wisdom burnt bright during the early Middle Ages. The tradition of the Grail and its spiritual Knighthood passed into literature through the hands of Chretien de Troyes, Wolfram von Eschenbach and other writers, whence on the one hand we derive the Morte d'Arthur of Sir Thomas Malory, from which Tennyson drew the materials for his Idylls of the King, and on the other the glorious music of Parsifal, in which Wagner reconstructed so magnificently the German tradition of the Grail Brotherhood.

Part XI:
Heredom

In Scotland these secret Mysteries of the East and West were handed down from generation to generation in various centres, one of the chief of these being the sacred island of Iona. Among the initiates of the Culdee rites Iona was called Heredom. Heredom is said in Masonic tradition to be a mystical mountain, and as such it is indeed the mount of Initiation beyond the veils of space and time; but it was also the secret name of the physical centre of the Mysteries - and this centre was Iona. Another such secret centre in mediaeval days was the Abbey of Kilwinning; and thus, the rites which derive in part from Culdee sources have always styled themselves as of Kilwinning and of Heredom.

The Saxon invasion of Britain drove the Celtic inhabitants of the plains to the mountains of the west and north; and thus there was a further mingling of the Jewish Mysteries of the Collegia with the Culdee rites. The Culdees of York were among the guardians of the Masonic tradition in the tenth century, and the Old Charges tell us that an assembly of Masons was held at York during the reign of King Athelstan, when a reorganization of the Craft took place. For many centuries York was a powerful centre of Masonry; and we have a curious piece of testimony given in 1835, by Godfrey Higgins, who claimed to be in possession of a Masonic document by which he could prove that "no very long time ago" the Culdees or Chaldaeans of York were Freemasons, that they constituted the Grand Lodge of England, and that they held their meetings in the crypt under the great cathedral of that city. (*Quoted in Waite's New Encyclopaedia, Art. Culdees.*) As we shall presently see, it was at York that certain important Masonic degrees emerged in the eighteenth century.

The monks of the Celtic Church were largely responsible for the introduction of Christianity into Germany. "Wherever they came they raised Churches and dwellings for their priests, cleared the forests, tilled the virgin soil, and instructed the heathen in the first principles of civilization. (*Gould. Hist. Freem., Vol. I, p. 107.*) Some German authorities have held that the monks directing these operations owed much of their success to the remnants of the Roman Colleges of Gaul and Britain, and ultimately laid the foundations of the craft guild system in Germany. Gould rejects this view on the ground that at the time of the Celtic influence there were no craft guilds in Germany; (*Gould. Hist. Freem., Vol. I, p. 109.*) but nevertheless some of the secret rites and traditions of the Celtic monks passed into the German monasteries and formed one of the lines of descent of those stonemasons who built the great German cathedrals in the Middle Ages.

In Scotland the Celtic Mystery-tradition passed down independently of the later operative Lodges, for there is no trace whatsoever of any high degrees in the extant Minutes of Mother Kilwinning, No. 0 upon the roll of the Grand Lodge of Scotland, which date from 1642. (*History of the Lodge of Edinburgh (Mary's Chapel, No. I) D. Murray Lyon, pp. 340, 434.*)

There is truth in the legend of the coming of certain of the French Knights Templars to Scotland after their proscription in 1307, and there was an intermingling of their doctrines also with the Scottish rites. One line of descent crossed from Scotland to France, where it was blended in the eighteenth century with the Egyptian tradition to form the rite of Heredom or of Perfection under the Council of the Emperors of the East and West. Another line was handed down in Scotland and England, becoming blended with Jewish Tradition, and Emerged in the Degrees of HRDM-RSYCS in what we now call the Royal Order of Scotland. The curious rhymed ritual of the Royal Order bears internal evidences of age, and although its Christianity has been ruthlessly edited in protestant interests there are yet traces of the old mystical ideas of the Celtic Church.

Operative Masonry in the Middle Ages
by C. W. Leadbeater
Part I:
The Temporary Custodians

In a complete study of mediaeval operative Masonry it would be necessary to include a treatise upon the various schools of mediaeval architecture and the tendencies, national and economic, which influenced their creation and development. In this book we are concerned with the operative builders only in so far as they were the temporary custodians of the speculative science of the Mysteries; but the study of architecture is of considerable value to the Mason; for it is the physical-plane reflection of mighty ideas in the inner worlds, and by the study of architecture certain of the laws of spiritual building may by analogy be reached and understood.

As Masons, our speculative ancestry is noble and magnificent, for we are in that respect the lineal descendants of the kings and prophets and priests of old who have been the bearers of the Hidden Light to men through countless generations; but of our operative forefathers who so faithfully guarded the tradition in the days of darkness we may also be proud, for their art at its zenith was unsurpassed in richness and splendour by the achievements of any other age in Europe; the great cathedrals and monasteries which they built to the glory of God and in the service of His Church are touched with the finger of divine inspiration, so that the cold marble is transfigured into almost unbelievable grace and delicacy; they are veritable dreams of beauty materialized into stone. The operative Masons, too, have handed down to us many of their customs and usages; and it is well that we should understand these in addition to what we have derived from other sources.

When Europe was overrun by the Germanic tribes and the Empire of the West was destroyed, the Roman Collegia for the most part disappeared with the other fruits of civilization. The Mysteries enshrined in them survived in a more or less repressed form in Italy, France and England, although they were kept extremely secret for fear of the barbarian invaders. It was from these survivals that the Lodges of the guild Masons of the Middle Ages were derived.

Part II:
Decline of Collegia

Mackey shows how the Collegia declined after the fall of Rome, and how new guilds were started and old ones revived under the patronage of the Christian clergy, and asserts that after the tenth century the whole of Europe was perambulated by bands of wanderers called Travelling Freemasons, who erected churches and monasteries in the Gothic style. Authorities differ seriously in opinion as to whether the fraternities who built the great cathedrals were joined together by any central organization. There is much in the similarity of style of building in the different countries, and in the Masonic signs upon the buildings, to indicate their connection, but the central organization must have allowed its branches great latitude, since the differences in style are also great. The cathedrals that the Travelling Freemasons built with such great skill and artistic inspiration were laid out upon a symbolic plan, usually based upon the cross and the vesica piscis, and there is some evidence that they moralized upon their tools. Undoubtedly these were men of the loftiest intellect and spirituality, and we modern speculative Masons have no reason to be ashamed of our associations with such operative craftsmen.

Part III:
The Comacini

The first signs of a revival in the art of building, the first stirrings of that creative spirit which was to blossom in later years in the full glory of the Gothic, are to be found in Lombardy, where originated the style called Romanesque, which eventually spread all over Europe. According to tradition, the College of Architects from Rome removed during the last days of the Empire to the safe refuge offered by the little republic of Comum, once the home of Pliny, and made its retreat upon the lovely island still known as Isola Comacina in Lake Como in Northern Italy. (*The Cathedral Builders, Leader Scott; pp. 11, 140.*) In A.D. 568 the surrounding country fell into the hands of the Lombards or Longobards, so-called from their long beards and uncouth appearance, whose original home had been in the lower basin of the Elbe; and although at first they were detested by the Italians, with surprising rapidity they developed enthusiasm for the arts and refinement of the land they had conquered. (*History of Art, H. B. Cotterill, Vol. I, p. 232.*)

The first mention in contemporary records of the celebrated Comacine Masters, who were descended from that Roman College, occurs in the code of the Lombard King Rothares (643), in which they figure as Master Masons with power to make contracts for building works and to employ workmen and labourers. (*The Cathedral Builders, p. 5.*) They are mentioned also in the Memoratorio of King Luitprand in 713,

(*Ibid., p. 24.*) when they received the privileges of freemen in the Lombard State. To their creative genius Romanesque architecture is due; and in all probability they adapted the traditional Roman methods to the requirements of their Lombard masters. It is clear from the Edict that they were highly-skilled architects. From a letter from Theodoric the Great to an architect whom he had appointed, we learn that the profession was highly developed, and an architect had to be able to construct a building from foundation to roof, and also decorate it with sculpture and painting, mosaic and bronzework. This inclusiveness prevailed in all the mediaeval schools up to 1335, when the Siennese painters seceded; and subsequently other branches also separated themselves into distinct guilds.

The first dawn of the new style (c. 600) was followed by a long period of obscuration, not unlike that Dark Age which in the evolution of Greek art followed the Dorian conquest. Then, with a strange suddenness, sprang forth (c. 1000) in wonderful perfection the new style, and rapidly extended itself over much of western and northern Christendom - the rapidity of this extension being easily explainable by the fact that master-builders and workmen were often summoned to great distances from well-known centres of architecture. In the same way as Venice and Ravenna sent to Constantinople for Byzantine builders, Charles the Great and many other princes, as well as cities, procured from Italy skilful Romanesque architects, such as the Comacine Masters, and the characteristics of this Lombard Romanesque are found not only in Germany and France but even in England. (*History of Art, Vol. I, p. 230.*)

Italian chroniclers relate that architects and builders were sent by Pope Gregory the Great to England with S. Augustine, and we learn from the Venerable Bede that S. Benedict Biscop set out for Gaul to search for masons to build the monastic church at Monk Wearmouth "according to the Roman style he had always loved". (*The Cathedral Builders, pp. 143, 154.*) S. Boniface visited Italy before undertaking his great mission to Germany in A.D. 715; Pope Gregory II gave him instructions and credentials, and sent with him a large following of monks versed in the art of building, and of lay brethren who were also architects to assist him. (*Ibid., p. 133.*) Leader Scott contends that these builders were Comacine Masters, and bases her arguments upon the evidence of building methods and the similarity of the styles employed. In like manner she traces the Comacini into France and Normandy, Southern Italy and Sicily, and even to Ireland in fact wherever the Romanesque style of building has penetrated.

Part IV:
The Comacine Lodges

The Comacine Guild not only inherited the building traditions of the Collegia, but also their secret Mysteries; and it was largely owing to the impulse given by them that a general revival of the existing Lodges of Europe took place. A very considerable interchange of influence occurs at this time; new Lodges were founded and old Lodges were restored, for, although the primary inspiration came from Italy, the builders in the different countries soon learnt to modify the new style in accordance with national requirements and taste. Many of the higher brethren, the Magistri of the Guild, were men of wide culture and refinement, who knew much of the inner meaning of the rites and ceremonies handed down amongst them; and it may well be that some among them possessed the knowledge now belonging to the higher degrees, for high degree signs are occasionally found upon their work. The majority of the craftsmen, however, probably knew little more than that there was a symbolical meaning to their ceremonies and tools, and tried to order their lives accordingly.

As Bro. J. S. M. Ward has pointed out very clearly, the Comacini show marked analogies with our modern Masonic system. They were organized into Masters and Disciples under the rule of a Gastaldo or Grand Master. Their working-places were called Lodges. They had Masters and Wardens, signs, tokens, grips, pass-words and oaths of secrecy and fidelity. The

Four Crowned Martyrs were their Patron Saints; they wore white aprons and gloves, and among the symbols associated with them we find the Lion of Judah, King Solomon's knot, the square and compasses, the level and plumb-rule, and the rose and compasses.

On a pulpit at Ravello, in one of their buildings of the thirteenth century, Jonah is seen coming out of the whale's mouth, making the F.C.H.S. (*Freemasonry and the Ancient Gods, J. S. M. Ward, Ch. xviii, passim.*) At Coire Cathedral in Switzerland, which is Romanesque in style and contains abundant evidence of Comacine work, several figures on the capitals of the pillars in the choir and sanctuary are depicted making Masonic s ... s, notably the F.C.H.S., the G. and R. S., and several s ... s, now associated with the Rose-Croix, Knights Templars, and other high degrees in Freemasonry. (*An Outline History of Freemasonry, J. S. M. Ward, p. 34.*) In the town-hall at Basle there is a fresco by Hans Dyg, painted in 1519, in which we may see the same s ... s, and also one of the Mark degree. King Solomon's knot is the traditional name among the Italians of today for the elaborate interlaced stonework executed by the Comacine Masters up to the eleventh century. It consists always of a single strand woven and interwoven in the most complex and beautiful designs. Leader Scott calls it "that intricate and endless variety of the single unbroken line of unity - emblem of the manifold ways of the power of the one God who has neither beginning nor end". (*The Cathedral Builders, p. 72.*)

Part V:
Other Survivals of the Collegia

Before passing on to the rise of Gothic architecture, which marks the climax of operative achievement in the Middle Ages, it will be well if we indicate certain other survivals of the Collegia and their Mysteries; for although the great impulse to restore the art of building came through the Comacine Masters, other Lodges had existed in Europe from Roman days which, under the influence of Italian inspiration, regained their power and vitality. In France especially it is clear that the organization of the Collegia was never fully destroyed and that the craft-guilds (Corps d'Etat) of the Middle Ages were derived from them in unbroken continuity.

The true origin of the corporation is found in the social life of the Romans, and amongst the vanquished Gauls, who always formed the principal population in the cities, and faithfully preserved under their new masters the remembrance and traces of their ancient organization. (*Levasseur, Histoire des Classes Ouvrieres en France, Vol. i, p. 104, quoted Gould i, p. 182.*)

Roman civil architecture, industry, art - in one word, the whole Roman tradition - was perpetuated in France till the tenth century. Even the German conquerors, while preserving their own national laws, customs, and usages, accepted the Gallic industry much as they found it. (*Monteil, Histoire de l'Industrie Francaise,* Preface by *C. Louandre, p. 76, quoted ibid., p. 183.)*

Not only was the trade organization preserved without break; the inner Mysteries of the Colleges of Architects were transmitted to the mediaeval building guilds of France, though they were no doubt strongly influenced by the Italian Masters who practiced the same Mysteries and the same glorious Craft.

Part VI:
The Compagnonnage

An interesting survival of the mediaeval craft-guilds of France is seen in an association of French journeymen for mutual support and assistance during their travels. Practically nothing was known about the practices of the Compagnonnage before the nineteenth century, although a partial revelation of one of the sections composing it (Enfants de Maitre Jacques) had been extracted by the Doctors of the Sorbonne in 1651, who not unnaturally stigmatized their proceedings as impiety and sacrilege. In 1841 the Livre du Compagnonnage was published by Agricol Perdiguier, a French workman of some culture, who undertook the task of revealing as much of the history and traditions of the Compagnonnage as his oath would permit, in order to put an end to the strife which ceaselessly occurred between its different sections.

The Compagnonnage consisted of three organizations perpetually at war with one another, each of which had an interesting traditional history and claimed a traditional chief. The oldest division was that of the Sons of Solomon, originally consisting of stonemasons only, although joiners and locksmiths were admitted later; the second was that of the Sons of Maitre Jacques, who likewise admitted members of these three trades and later of many others, notably saddlers, shoemakers, tailors, cutlers, and hatters; while the third section followed Maitre Soubise, and was originally composed only of carpenters, although at a later date plasterers and tilers were also admitted. It is generally conceded that the Sons of Solomon were the oldest of all; and another remarkable fact is that the masons (to be carefully distinguished from the Stonemasons) were never admitted at all. Houses of call belonging to these three associations existed in the more important towns of France; and travelling journeymen had the right to lodging and assistance in finding work in the houses belonging to their fraternity.

The three sections of the Compagnonnage preserved legends concerning King Solomon and his temple. Little is known of the form of the legend current among the Sons of Solomon, but there are curious indications that the story of the death of Hiram (which is not contained in the Bible) was known to them. Perdiguier tells us little, but he gives certain hints:

An ancient fable has obtained currency amongst them (the Sons of Solomon) relating, according to some, to Hiram, according to others, to Adonhiram; wherein are represented crimes and punishments. Again he tells us "that the joiners of Maitre Jacques wear white gloves, because, as they say, they did not steep their hands in the blood of Hiram."

Furthermore with regard to the use of the word chien bestowed upon all the Compagnons du Devoir, he says:

It is believed by some to be derived from the fact that it was a dog which discovered the place where the body of Hiram, architect of the Temple, lay under the rubbish, after which all the companions who separated from the murderers of Hiram were called chiens or dogs.

Some have thought, and among them Perdiguier himself, that these are indications of a legend which may have been borrowed from the Freemasons; but they clearly point to an independent line of tradition handed down among the stonemasons of France. Maitre Jacques and Maitre Soubise have also their traditional histories, likewise going back to the days of Solomon's Temple; and in that of the former an elaborate account of the death of Maitre Jacques is given, which may likewise be an echo of the death of another and greater Master - for it is clearly intended to be symbolical. There is also a suggestion that it was taken to refer to the death of Jacques de Molay, the last Grand Master of the Knights Templars. Much yet remains to be discovered about the Compagnonnage, for no full investigation into its records has yet taken place; and it may well be that future research will show clearly that the speculative Masons of England and the operative journeymen of France derive their traditions from a common ancestry in the ancient Mysteries. This at least was the opinion of R. F. Gould, the greatest of our Masonic historians. (*See Gould. Hist. Freem., Vol. I, ch. iv and v, for a complete account of what is known of the French Craft Guilds and the Compagnonnage.*)

Part VII:
The Stonemasons of Germany

Another line of survival of the ancient tradition is found among the Stonemasons of Germany. We have already traced the influence of two streams of tradition into Germany, one emanating from Britain through the Celtic monks, and another coming from Italy through S. Boniface. The craft guilds of Germany developed independently of monastic influence, but according to Gould it is probable that in the twelfth century the skilled masons of the monasteries amalgamated with the craft builders in the towns, and together formed the society afterwards known throughout Germany as the Steinmetzen. (*Concise History of Freemasonry*, R. F. Gould, p. 17.)

We know from the Torgau Ordinances of 1462 that the Stonemasons venerated the Four Crowned Martyrs as their patron saints, and the Strasburg Constitutions of 1459 contain a devout invocation of the names of the "Father, Son, and Holy Ghost; of our gracious Mother Mary; and of her blessed servants, the Holy Four Crowned Martyrs of everlasting memory". (*Gould, Concise History, p. 19.*) From the Brother-Book of 1563 we learn that they had a greeting and a grip which might not be described in writing; (*Gould, Hist. of Freem., Vol. i, p. 128.*) and a curious piece of testimony came to light at the beginning of the nineteenth century, when a certain architect, who had joined a survival of the Stonemasons and was subsequently admitted into Masonry, recognized the E.A. grip as identical with that of the Steinmetzen of Strasburg. (*Ibid., p. 146.*) A ceremony of admission was in use among them; but what it was is not known. (*Concise History, Gould, p. 22.*)

At Daberan in Mecklenburg there is a carving of the Last Supper, wherein the apostles are depicted in well-known Masonic attitudes, (*An Outline History of Freemasonry, J. S. M. Ward, p. 35.*) while according to the Bulletin of the Supreme Council of the Ancient and Accepted Scottish Rite (Southern Jurisdiction, U.S.A.) the legend of Hiram Abiff is carved in stone at Strasburg. (*Op, cit., vii, 200.*) In the cathedral at Wurzburg two pillars, inscribed Jachin and Boaz, originally stood at the porchway or entrance, but they have now been moved within the building. Stieglitz in his Early German Architecture says that they were intended to bear a symbolic reference to the fraternity. (*Gould, Concise Hist., p. 24.*) A bas-relief in a convent near Schaffhausen depicts a figure making one of the s ... s of an I.M. (*An Outline History of Freemasonry, J. S. M. Ward, p. 11.*) In the year 1459 the Stonemasons of Germany united to form a Grand Guild, governed by four Head Lodges, of which Strasburg was the chief. So close are the parallels between its organization and that of modern speculative Masonry that many German writers have held that the Steinmetzen were the originators of the speculative system. As a matter of fact there appears to have been no interchange in modern times between the two corporations, and modern German Craft Masonry is clearly derived from England. (*Gould, Concise History, pp. 18, 24.*)

Part VIII:
The English Guilds

Three distinct lines of tradition contribute to the Masonry of the English guilds. One line was preserved among the Celts, as we have already seen, and became mingled in later times with streams from other sources. Secondly, the Roman Collegia survived to some extent in England after the departure of the Romans; the Saxons found them there and did not interfere with them. (*Coote - cited in The Cathedral Builders, Leader Scott, p. 140.*) Thirdly, there was the influx of Continental builders, beginning in the time of S. Augustine, but greatly augmented after the Norman Conquest under the patronage of Archbishop Lanfranc, the first Norman Archbishop of Canterbury, a Lombard by birth and a celebrated patron of building even before he came to England. (*J. S. M. Ward, Freemasonry and the Ancient Gods, p. 147.*) All these streams of tradition were represented in the mediaeval guilds, and were handed down in various centres. The French craft-guilds preserve accounts similar to those found in our English Old Charges regarding the assistance given to Masons by Charles Martel. (*Gould, Concise History, p. 30.*)

The secret Mysteries of the Craft, common, save for certain unimportant local modifications, to all these lines of descent, Celtic, Saxon and Continental, were handed down in the Lodges of the mediaeval Masons, which were the units of organization and labour within the guilds; they were never written down, but were transmitted orally from generation to generation, the succession passing down from Master to Master as in the present day. The primary work of the Lodges was of course operative, and the speculative ritual which was handed drown so faithfully in essentials was regarded as an ancient heritage to be scrupulously transmitted to posterity; but it is unlikely that any but the few recognized its true purpose, or thought of it as containing more than a merely moral code of life. It is due to the rigid observance of the O. "never to write those secrets" (an O. which would have been enforced by certain pains and penalties not unknown to Masons today), that no trace of the ritual can be found in any document prior to 1717; and it is because of this lack of all records that many Masonic scholars believe that it was compiled only at the beginning of the eighteenth century. Even in the fourteenth and fifteenth centuries, when the Old Charges were written down, no mention is made of the Legend of Hiram; for this formed part of the secret ritual and therefore might not be divulged. A figure representing God the Son in the porch of Peterborough Cathedral is depicted as making the F.C.H.S. (*J. S. M. Ward, Op. cit., p. 116.*) showing that this s ... at least was known to our old operative brethren.

Part IX:
The Rise of Gothic Architecture

The climax of mediaeval operative building was reached in the twelfth and thirteenth centuries in the rise and development of Gothic architecture, which was inspired directly by the Head of all true Freemasons throughout the world, as part of the plan for the development of the fifth or Teutonic sub-race. Many theories have been advanced to account for the rapid development of the new style.

Whether the wonderful change of style that in a few years spread over a great part of Western Christendom was due primarily to the discovery of the possibilities of the pointed arch or those of the so-called ogival vaulting is much disputed. Probably it was due to both, and also of course to certain movements, social and political, which were bound to favour immensely any such new enthusiasm; for a new national consciousness was rapidly gaining strength, especially in France, and cities and communes were beginning to vie in erecting vast buildings - first cathedrals and later civic edifices - the architects being now mostly laymen, the founders and donors often municipal bodies and rich citizens, and the workmen not seldom volunteers from the people. The old monastic era of Romanesque suddenly gave way to that of a new, popular, and civic architecture, and in a surprisingly short time much the same had happened as that which we noted after the passing of the fateful year A.D. 1000, when, according to old Raoul Glaber, Christendom cast aside its outworn attire and put on a fresh white robe of new-built Churches. (*Cotterill, History of Art, Vol. I, p. 278.*)

We, however, do not need to speculate or theorize as to the causes of the rapid development of the new style, for we have the advantage of knowing that the movement was all the time being definitely steered from behind by the H.O.A.T.F. and a corps of able assistants under his direction.

As I have already said, architecture has a powerful effect upon the consciousness of the people, for it is one of the means chosen by the White Lodge to influence the development of the various nations according to the plan of the Great Architect of the Universe. To understand the significance of the Gothic style, we must consider for a moment an important fact of occult history, that which is technically known to students as the cyclic change of Ray. The seven rays, or types of the divine consciousness and activity, to one or other of which all living things belong, influence the world in turn, and this cyclic change produces the modifications of outlook which are to be noted as century succeeds century.

Each race and sub-race has its own especial qualities to develop. The fifth root-race, to which we ourselves belong, is engaged as a whole in the unfolding of intellect; but each of its sub-races has likewise a quality to cultivate. The fourth or Celtic sub-race was concerned with the evolution of intellect through the emotions, and so produced the beauty-loving peoples whom we see in Greece and Ireland; while the fifth or Teutonic sub-race, to which the Anglo-Saxons and Scandinavians belong, is striving to awaken the intellect working in the concrete mind, and so is producing the scientific and industrial nations which lead the world today.

This cyclic change of Ray, which is also part of the great plan, produces other, but no less definite modifications in the corporate consciousness. In Greece we saw something of the fifth ray, the ray of knowledge, working upon the fourth sub-race with its love of beauty, resulting in that intellectual type of art so characteristic of the classical age; the Middle Ages show forth the qualities of the sixth ray, the ray of devotion, working upon the fifth or Teutonic sub-race, and producing as its characteristic intellectual fruit scholastic philosophy with its hair-splitting intellectuality based upon an almost fanatical devotion.

Devotion, indeed, was the great characteristic of the Middle Ages. The twelfth and thirteenth centuries, so rich in the annals of Christian mysticism, were adorned by men and women whose power of devotion reached heights rarely touched in any other age. The great S. Bernard (who among many other noted works gave their Rule to the Order of Knights Templars), Richard of S. Victor, S. Hildegarde, S. Francis of Assisi and S. Antony of Padua, and a little later S. Bonaventura and S. Thomas Aquinas - all these have shone forth as a light unto many generations. Profound changes took place in the Catholic Church during these significant years, and Europe rose from the dark ages into the full glory of an era of culture and art. Gothic architecture was intended to lift the devotion of the masses to greater heights than had been induced by the contemplation of the flatter Romanesque style; by its soaring lines and ever-ascending curves, by the richness of its ornamentation and the splendid complexity of its design, by its amazing grace and delicacy, it had power to raise the hearts of men on the wings of its silent music to the very throne of God Himself, to mold and enrich their devotion in unseen subtle ways, to pour out upon them spiritual influences which would aid in the great work of transformation which had to be accomplished.

The change from Romanesque to Gothic, then, was brought about deliberately. The inspiration was given to certain master-builders in the different countries by the H.O.A.T.F., and the erection of the splendid cathedrals of the period was carried out by travelling bands of Masons passing from centre to centre, and doubtless employing the local builders upon the actual work of construction. This, as we have said, was an age of devotion, and every stone was carved with the utmost care to the glory of God, and thereby charged with the adoration of the skilful craftsmen who worked so unselfishly. The powerful spiritual influences generated by all this loving care have contributed in no small degree to the extraordinary beauty of the Gothic cathedrals, and to the power which they possess even in the present day of evoking devotion and reverence from all who approach them.

The particular expressions of Gothic vary in the different countries, and even in different parts of the same country; that is always the case in every style of building. But behind the whole order of Gothic architecture there is one great idea, that of soaring, passionate devotion ever rising to the feet of God; and that is found with national modifications in England, France, Germany, Italy and Spain. This was the great age of operative Masonry, and at its close the building corporations began to decline in power, until in England and Germany especially the movement miscalled the Reformation killed out ecclesiastical architecture, and church building as a fine art practically ceased.

In the fourteenth century the merchant guilds, which organized an entire industry, became decentralized, and a new system of craft guilds gradually arose, organizing different branches of each industry. This change of organization was due to a profound change of thought among the people, which was to lead to the great stirring of the Renaissance and the growth of national consciousness in the different countries. It is at this period that the Old Charges of our ancient operative Brn. first appear, and they were written down as the Freemasons became gradually disorganized, in order to preserve the older oral records from oblivion.

Part X:
The Old Charges

These Old Charges reflect in no small measure the ignorance of the time in matters of geography and chronology, but they nevertheless contain an account of the broad outline of Masonic descent from Egypt, through Judaea, into Europe; and it would certainly be difficult to suppose that they were fabricated by mere operative builders who had nothing of hidden mystery to transmit. I give below a brief summary of the Dowland manuscript, which is fairly representative of the tradition common to all. It is reproduced from Hughan's Old Charges (1872), and is quoted from Mackey's Encyclopaedia. (*Art. Legend of the Craft.*)

The legend begins with an account of Lamech and his four children, who founded all the sciences of the world before the flood. These sciences were engraved on two pillars, one of which was later found by Hermes, who taught its contents to the people. Nimrod is next mentioned as having employed Masons at the building of the Tower of Babel, and as having given them their first Charge. Next Abraham and Sarah are said to have taught the seven sciences to the Egyptians, and especially to a "worthy Scoller that hight Ewclyde". The latter was commissioned by the king to teach Masonry to a large number of children of "the lord and estates of the realm". The legend passes then to David, who, when he began the temple of Jerusalem, learned the Charges and manners of Masons from Egypt and gave them to his people. Solomon continued the building of the temple after David's death, sent for Masons from all lands, and confirmed the Charges given by his father. There is no reference to the legend of the 3° in any of the Old Charges before the second edition of Anderson's Constitutions, published in 1738, except that Aynon, the son of Iram, is mentioned as being the "chiefe Maister" of all Masons, and "Master of all his gravings and carvinge and of all other manner of Masonrye that longed to the temple". The legend, in defiance of all chronology, then states that, "one curious Mason that hight Maymus Grecus", who had been at the making of Solomon's temple, taught Masonry to Charles Martel of France. Since the latter died in A.D. 741, the former would have been about seventeen hundred years old, unless we are to understand that the Charge assumes that he had reincarnated!

A legendary account is given of S. Albans work for Masons in the third century, and especially of his institution of General Assemblies. He is also said to have obtained for them a Charter, to have given them Charges, and to have arranged for better pay. Later, Athelstan is said to have built many abbeys and towers, and to have "loved well masons". His son Edwin, who loved them still more, held an Assembly at York and gave them a Charter. All the old writings were collected at this period, "some in Frenche, and some in Greek, and some in English, and some in other languages; and the intent of them all was founded all one". These old writings were digested into the York Constitutions which resulted from this Assembly of A.D. 926. It is from this source that we draw the material now embodied in the Old Charges.

www.ingramcontent.com/pod-product-compliance
Lightning Source LLC
LaVergne TN
LVHW041457070426
835507LV00009B/653